KRISS KROSS PUZZLES FOR KIDS
EXCITING UNUSUAL GAME FOR CHILDREN 5-10 YEARS OLD
CRISS CROSS BOOK

Contents:

Instruction - 2
Kriss Kross Puzzles - 3
Solutions - 53

Instruction:

To complete the puzzle you should place all the words inside the grid. This is only one way to fit all the words. If you fail, you can see the answers at the back.

Copyright © **Brain Revolution** 2021

Kriss Kross № 1

5 letter word
Toast

7 letter words
Netting
Trumpet

9 letter words
Bicycling
Columbine
Forelimbs
Positives

10 letter words
Indigenous
Intimation
Intonation
Prevailing
Vaudeville

11 letter words
Exquisitely
Objectivity
Orientation

Kriss Kross № 2

4 letter word
Stay

5 letter words
Cadre
Light
Weeds

6 letter words
Shears
Vector

7 letter words
Glasses
Petunia
Updates

8 letter word
Artifice

9 letter words
Assurance
Dirigible
Socialism

10 letter word
Credential

11 letter word
Supposition

Kriss Kross № 3

4 letter words
Loom
Raft

5 letter word
Thuja

6 letter words
Action
Aronia
Runner

7 letter word
Persona

8 letter words
Activity
Cleavage
Simulate

9 letter words
Empirical
Migration
Pacifying

11 letter word
Cognoscente

12 letter word
Similarities

Kriss Kross № 4

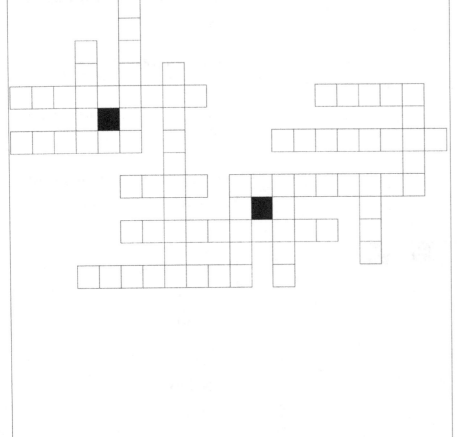

4 letter words
Ford
Knit

5 letter words
Beans
Blues
Sight
Thank
Triad

6 letter word
Cooked

7 letter word
Updated

8 letter words
Reflexes
Servings

9 letter words
Butterfat
Tarantula

10 letter words
Evaluation
Illuminate

Kriss Kross № 5

4 letter words
Jaws
Play

5 letter words
Irons
Madam
Penny
Pesky
Skill

6 letter words
Bearer
Replay
Taylor

7 letter words
Cicadas
Lincoln

9 letter words
Punchwork
Repentant

12 letter word
Intermediary

Kriss Kross № 6

4 letter words
Grin
Iran
Pita

5 letter words
Chime
Fiber
Stock

6 letter words
Pounds
Powder
Summer
Wooden

7 letter word
Winning

9 letter words
Abolition
Buttercup
Criterion

11 letter word
Forbearance

Kriss Kross № 7

4 letter words
Make
Pony

6 letter words
Honest
Hyphen
Supine

7 letter words
Beetles
Dangers
Vietnam

8 letter words
Allusion
Firewall
Shavings

9 letter words
Filmmaker
Ponderous
Repeating

10 letter word
Theatrical

Kriss Kross № 8

4 letter words
Free
Nick

5 letter words
Speed
Tuber

6 letter words
Nurses
Target

7 letter words
Husband
Migrate
Palette

8 letter words
Cheerful
Elegance
Portrait

9 letter word
Cyclopean

10 letter words
Broomstick
Theologian

Kriss Kross № 9

4 letter word
Ward

5 letter words
Cards
Washy

6 letter words
Buster
Genera
Quotes
Tablet

7 letter words
Charter
Courtly
Forearm

8 letter words
Feasible

Jongleur
Juggling

10 letter word
Spectators

11 letter word
Conditioner

Kriss Kross № 10

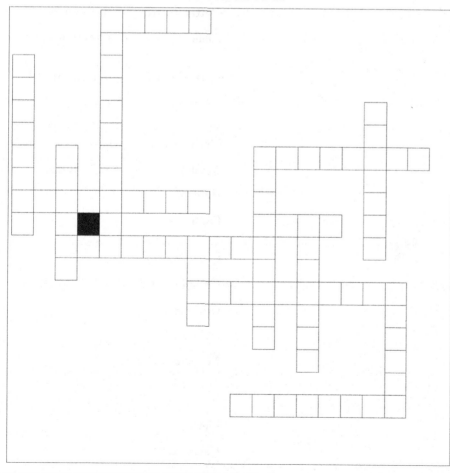

4 letter words
Nest
Rate

5 letter word
Manor

6 letter words
Imbibe
Turkey

7 letter words
Figures
Samples

8 letter words
Brownish
Maturity
Packages

9 letter words
Paintings
Sobriquet

10 letter words
Breakfront
Transplant

11 letter word
Materialize

Kriss Kross № 11

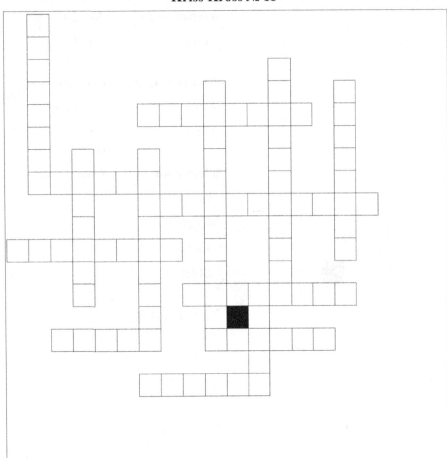

5 letter words
Axles
Lewis

6 letter words
Gather
Joyous
Seller

7 letter word
Stature

8 letter words
Donation
Migrants
Sizzling
Upturned
Whiskers

9 letter word
Trapezius

11 letter words
Appreciated
Ultraviolet

12 letter word
Preparations

Kriss Kross № 12

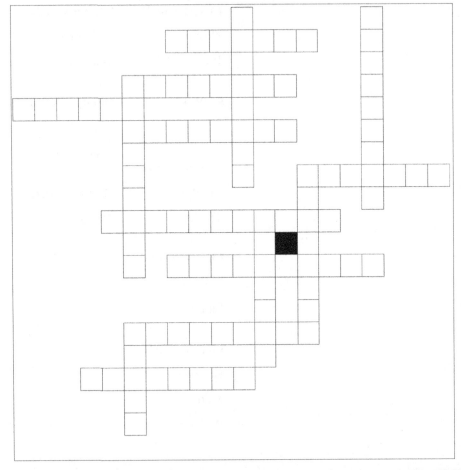

5 letter word
Khaki

6 letter word
Cinema

7 letter words
Acquire
Helipad
Picture

8 letter words
Colonies
Creative
Guaranty
Musician
Puritans

9 letter words
Cacophony
Kilograms
Labyrinth

10 letter word
Insulators

11 letter word
Forefathers

Kriss Kross № 13

6 letter words
Cooler
Shield

7 letter words
Effects
Foodies
Impulse
Outback
Runners

8 letter words
Capitals
Kinetics
Magazine
Volcanic

9 letter word
Perpetual

10 letter words
Easterlies
Inflatable
Obligation

Kriss Kross № 14

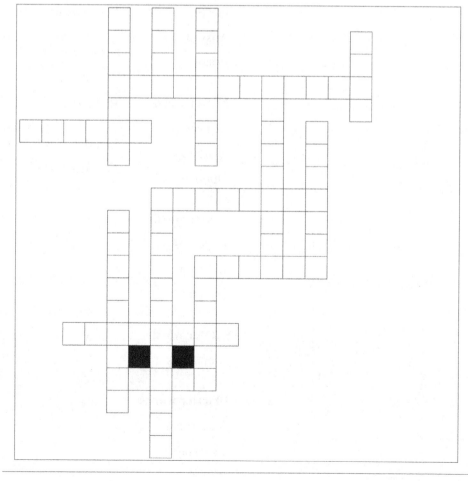

4 letter words
Gait
Zing

5 letter word
Cells

6 letter words
Charts
Colors
Lemony

7 letter words
Canyons
Closing
Sensual

8 letter words
Rapidity
Reaction

9 letter words
Abundance
Caregiver

12 letter words
Recapitulate
Satisfaction

Kriss Kross № 15

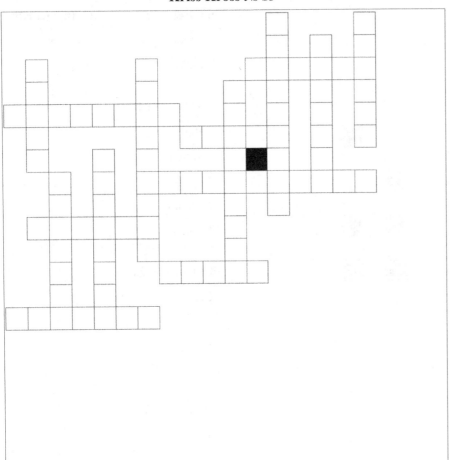

5 letter words
Acids
Blank
Dream

6 letter words
Decade
Fallow
Rustic

7 letter words
Charges
Fishing
Statute

8 letter words
Kohlrabi
Renowned

9 letter words
Animation
Overgrown
Youngster

11 letter word
Replacement

Kriss Kross № 16

6 letter words
Answer
Prices

7 letter words
Collect
Headway
Optimal

8 letter words
Expenses
Lifeboat
Literary

9 letter word
Merchants

10 letter words
Reinforces
Skyscraper

Sportswear

11 letter words
Aftermarket
Inclination

12 letter word
Construction

Kriss Kross № 17

4 letter word
Toot

5 letter words
Sauna
Unite
Wired

6 letter words
Cabana
Canter
Jockey
Varied
Weasel

7 letter word
Utility

8 letter words
Numerous

Progress
Spinning

9 letter word
Handicaps

12 letter word
Entrepreneur

Kriss Kross № 18

4 letter word
Diet

5 letter word
Calls

6 letter words
Decree
Digest
Mumble
Subway

7 letter words
Clutter
Convert
Culture
Popular

8 letter word
Downpour

9 letter words
Connector
Unselfish

11 letter word
Cooperation

12 letter word
Spectroscope

Kriss Kross № 19

4 letter words
Aqua
Sane
Teas

6 letter words
Queens
Ruckus

7 letter words
Beanbag
Organic

8 letter words
Advisors
Columbus
Hibiscus
Vaulting

9 letter words
Birthdays
Sunbather

10 letter words
Archeology
Folklorist

Kriss Kross № 20

4 letter word
Side

5 letter word
Ebony

6 letter word
Helium

7 letter words
America
Predict

8 letter words
Readings
Shelving
Unguenta

9 letter words
Backyards
Battalion
Homograph

10 letter words
Dependable
Meadowlark

11 letter words
Citizenship
Comfortable

Kriss Kross № 21

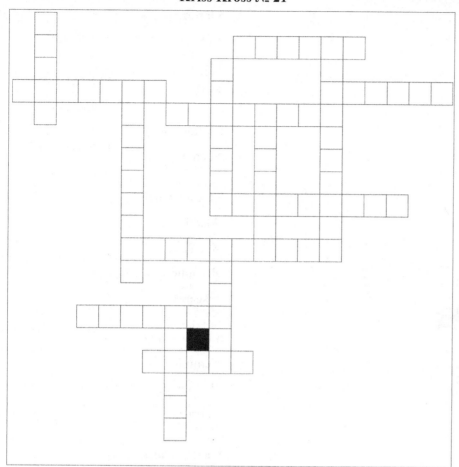

5 letter words
Feast
Libel

6 letter words
Caviar
Exodus
Horses
Plenty

7 letter words
Bequest
Bromine
Element
Whipped

8 letter word
Slovenia

9 letter words

Exercises
Sasquatch

10 letter words
Correction
Escalation

Kriss Kross № 22

4 letter words
Goat
Sock

5 letter words
Broad
Italy
Seeds
Voice

6 letter words
Bumper
Retire
Spades

7 letter words
Convent
Valency

9 letter words

Candlemas
Impartial

10 letter words
Prominence
Reputation

13

Kriss Kross № 23

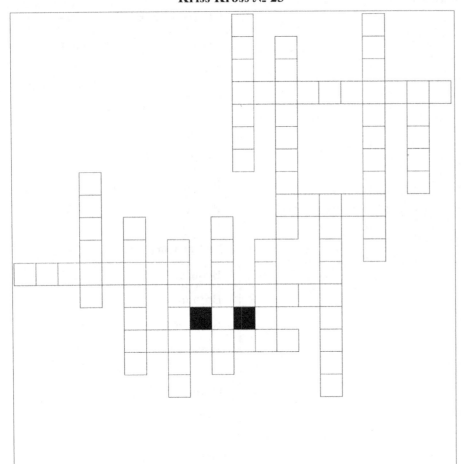

5 letter words
Libre
Mount
Ocean

6 letter word
Scenic

7 letter words
Aladdin
Knights
Perfume
Seasons

8 letter words
Feminine
Redouble
Tourists

9 letter words
Bettering
Brotherly

10 letter word
Stonemason

11 letter word
Enlargement

Kriss Kross № 24

5 letter words
Cache
Plank
Polar

6 letter words
Chance
Crunch

7 letter words
Marshal
Striped

8 letter words
Exercise
Stalwart
Taxation

9 letter words
Fisherman
Navigable
Suspected

10 letter word
Reflection

11 letter word
Grandmother

Kriss Kross № 25

4 letter words
Heat
Site

5 letter word
Lands

6 letter word
Equity

7 letter words
Dolores
Inkblot

8 letter words
Adjutant
Attorney
Coverlet
Grouping
Hallmark

Porthole
Punching

9 letter word
Curiosity

10 letter word
Beatitudes

Kriss Kross № 26

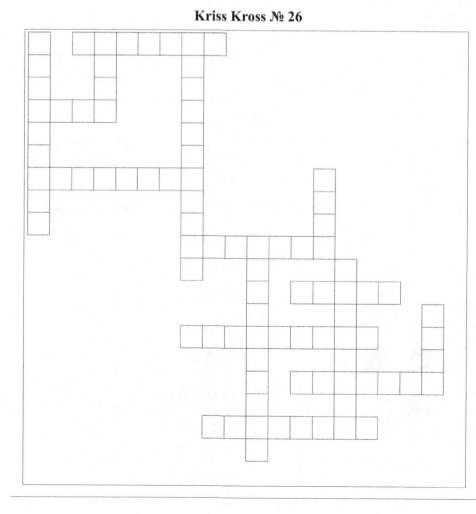

4 letter words
Core
Envy
Odds
Vows

5 letter word
Fluke

7 letter words
Chicory
Colloid
Example

8 letter words
Applique
Function
Munching

9 letter words
Forensics
Gravitate

10 letter word
Mastermind

11 letter word
Intercepted

Kriss Kross № 27

5 letter words
Agree
Chute
Paten
Satin
Youth

6 letter words
Gadget
Roping

7 letter words
Auction
Bonding

8 letter words
Flatland
Seraphim

9 letter words

Liquidity
Matrimony
Newspaper

11 letter word
Refurbished

Kriss Kross № 28

4 letter word
Hood

6 letter words
Curing
Linger
Savoir

7 letter words
Manhole
Oranges
Receipt

8 letter word
Modulate

9 letter words
Maladroit
Observing
Outspoken

10 letter words
Dependence
Futuristic

11 letter word
Compliments

12 letter word
Subterranean

Kriss Kross № 29

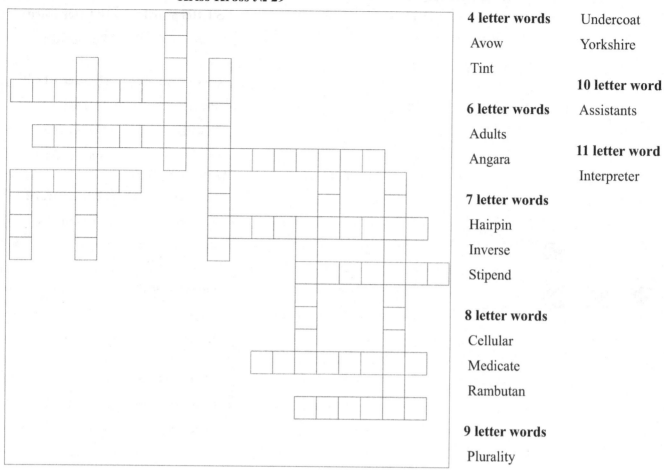

4 letter words
Avow
Tint

6 letter words
Adults
Angara

7 letter words
Hairpin
Inverse
Stipend

8 letter words
Cellular
Medicate
Rambutan

9 letter words
Plurality

Undercoat
Yorkshire

10 letter word
Assistants

11 letter word
Interpreter

Kriss Kross № 30

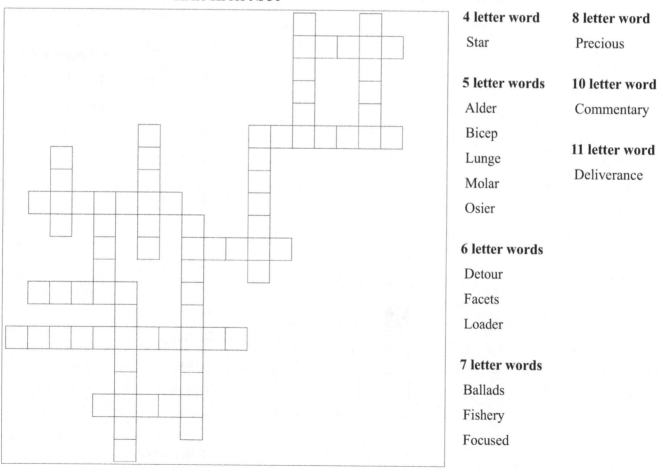

4 letter word
Star

5 letter words
Alder
Bicep
Lunge
Molar
Osier

6 letter words
Detour
Facets
Loader

7 letter words
Ballads
Fishery
Focused

8 letter word
Precious

10 letter word
Commentary

11 letter word
Deliverance

Kriss Kross № 31

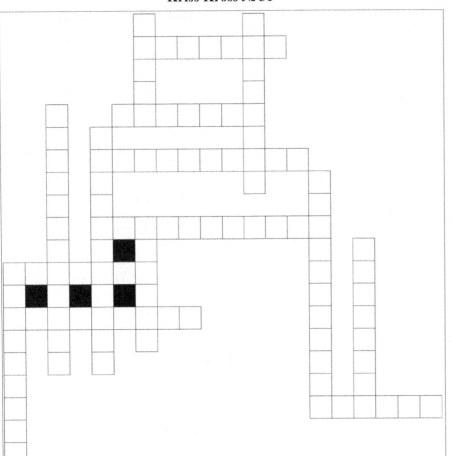

5 letter word
Trust

6 letter words
Precis
Sheath

7 letter words
Relaxer
Salvage
Student

8 letter words
Curative
Relation

9 letter words
Collision
Succulent

10 letter word
Euphonious

11 letter words
Enthusiasts
Legislation
Supermarket

12 letter word
Unparalleled

Kriss Kross № 32

4 letter word
Hike

5 letter words
Fugue
Pooch
Steve

6 letter word
Styles

7 letter words
Angling
Miracle
Seafood
Valiant
Various
Wealthy

8 letter word
Diaspora

9 letter words
Elucidate
Rejoinder
Welcoming

Kriss Kross № 33

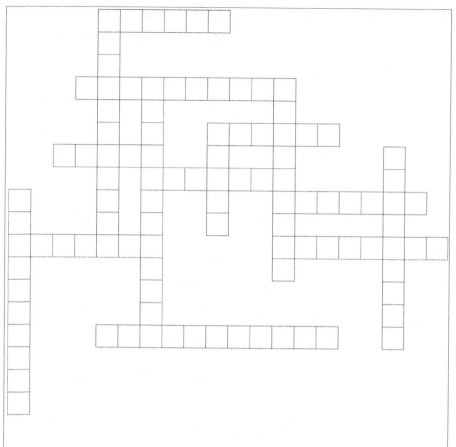

5 letter words
Belts
Bound

6 letter words
Blooms
Garble

7 letter words
England
Federal
Hunters

8 letter word
Sporting

9 letter words
Stability
Swordfish

10 letter words
Stupendous
Upholstery

11 letter words
Gesticulate
Reservation

12 letter word
Predecessors

Kriss Kross № 34

4 letter word
Holy

5 letter word
Maria

6 letter words
Active
Assets
Batter
Gabled
Patrol

7 letter words
Matches
Radiant

8 letter word
Workable

9 letter word
Magnitude

10 letter words
Assistance
Boondoggle
Zoological

11 letter word
Furnishings

Kriss Kross № 35

4 letter word
Fuzz

5 letter word
Rails

6 letter words
Ending
London
Salvia

7 letter words
Beloved
Chopped
Pacific

8 letter words
Homespun
Petulant
Stuffing

9 letter word
Exclusive

10 letter words
Repertoire
Underwater

12 letter word
Antananarivo

Kriss Kross № 36

5 letter words
Cider
Swiss

6 letter words
Acumen
Sliver
Sophia
Summon

7 letter words
Flutter
Fulfill
Galette
Grenada
Slavery

9 letter word
Fortunate

10 letter word
Fieldstone

11 letter words
Candlelight
Tragicomedy

Kriss Kross № 37

4 letter words
Fuel
Ways

5 letter words
Dakar
Eager

6 letter words
Nebula
Paired
Spongy

7 letter words
Elation
Regalia

8 letter words
Presence
Tailgate

9 letter words
Nostalgia
Organisms

10 letter word
Toiletries

12 letter word
Quintessence

Kriss Kross № 38

4 letter words
Fawn
Tale

5 letter words
Hooks
Steps

6 letter words
Malawi
Pueblo

8 letter words
Checkers
Stripped
Takeover

9 letter word
Sunscreen

10 letter words
Compromise
Ventilator

11 letter word
Mendelssohn

12 letter words
Memorization
Plainclothes

Kriss Kross № 39

4 letter words
Aman
Emit
Mugs

5 letter word
Exact

6 letter words
Aerial
Choked
Glossy
Mirror

7 letter words
Captive
Natives

8 letter word
Rhapsody

9 letter words
Gallantry
Microwave

11 letter words
Homogeneous
Precautions

Kriss Kross № 40

5 letter words
Godly
Organ

6 letter words
Cloths
Pampus
Waving

7 letter words
Annuity
Country
Pension
Scarves

9 letter words
Academics
Bracelets
Essential

10 letter words
Permission
Tantamount

11 letter word
Grandfather

Kriss Kross № 41

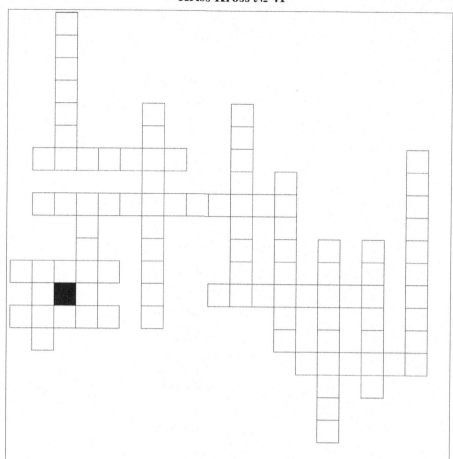

4 letter word
Isle

5 letter words
Plush
Vivid

6 letter words
Fluids
Rivers

7 letter words
Decades
Pointer
Program

8 letter words
Hermetic
Newcomer

9 letter words
Materials
Rectangle

10 letter words
Craftiness
Goaltender

12 letter word
Affectionate

Kriss Kross № 42

4 letter words
Arms
Icon
Pray

5 letter words
Comet
Lathe
Tulle

6 letter word
Lilies

8 letter words
Birdcage
Conjugal
Proposal

9 letter words
Hydroxide
Incidence
Wrestling

10 letter word
Continuing

12 letter word
Recuperation

Kriss Kross № 43

4 letter word
Rein

5 letter words
Cumin
Exalt

6 letter words
Arabic
Callow
Gerund
Mussel

8 letter words
Activism
Repartee
Scholars

9 letter words
Socialist

Versatile

10 letter words
Foreground
Jubilation

11 letter word
Monasteries

Kriss Kross № 44

4 letter words
Fact
Mali

6 letter words
Iodine
Thanks

7 letter words
Abdomen
Captain
Grownup
Promote

8 letter words
Blockade
Striving

10 letter words
Cladistics

Diminutive

11 letter words
Crepuscular
Netherlands

12 letter word
Inauguration

Kriss Kross № 45

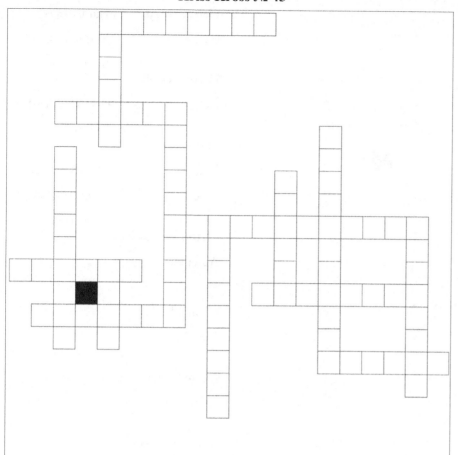

4 letter word
Sing

6 letter words
Classy
Diving
Picked
Speech
Wisdom

7 letter word
Magnify

8 letter words
Emigrate
Reverend
Soothing

9 letter words
Breakaway

Motorboat

10 letter word
Dependency

11 letter word
Waterlogged

12 letter word
Demonstrator

Kriss Kross № 46

4 letter words
Pots
Wind

6 letter words
Camels
Detect

7 letter words
Fashion
Flowery
Prolong

8 letter word
Sequence

9 letter word
Waterfowl

10 letter words

Exobiology
Subjective
Unplayable

11 letter words
Achievement
Charismatic
Questioning

Kriss Kross № 47

4 letter word
Hymn

5 letter word
Ocher

6 letter words
Junket
Woodsy

7 letter words
Antenna
Bedroll
Channel
Marches

9 letter word
Anonymous

10 letter words
Hamstrings
Maturation
Semicircle

11 letter word
Indivisible

12 letter words
Conservatory
Positiveness

Kriss Kross № 48

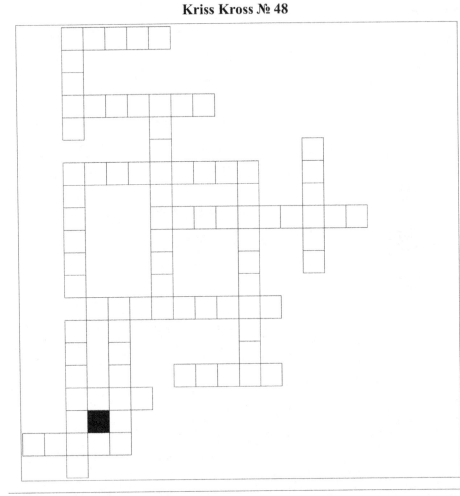

4 letter word
Hall

5 letter words
Barge
Daisy
Deuce
Druid

6 letter words
Moving
Pigeon

7 letter words
Devalue
Showers
Wishful

9 letter words
Adenosine
Penurious

10 letter words
Conformity
Extraction
Shortening

Kriss Kross № 49

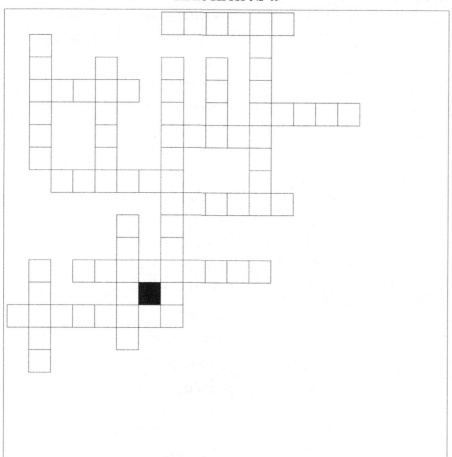

4 letter word
Army

5 letter words
Bring
Egypt
Slush
Wines

6 letter words
Candid
Header
Reward
Soften
Torque
Unripe

8 letter word
Kinesics

9 letter words
Lingering
Palestine

12 letter word
Timelessness

Kriss Kross № 50

5 letter word
Motor

6 letter words
Chaste
Mallet

7 letter words
Kidding
Respite

8 letter words
Academic
Campsite
Glissade
Infantry
Possible

9 letter words
Epitomise
Resonance

10 letter words
Counseling
Solidarity

11 letter word
Magnanimous

Kriss Kross № 51

4 letter word
Vila

6 letter word
Riddle

7 letter words
Lasagna
Optical
Platter
Powered

8 letter words
Attached
Hedgehog
Nearside
Shouting

9 letter words
Cessation

Gestation
Immensity
Masculine

11 letter word
Sustainable

Kriss Kross № 52

5 letter word
Vista

6 letter words
Reader
Sprout
Subaru

7 letter words
Daycare
Linking

8 letter word
Research

9 letter words
Bodyguard
Democracy
Inventing

10 letter word
Repentance

11 letter words
Attachments
Compartment
Convocation

12 letter word
Friendliness

Kriss Kross № 53

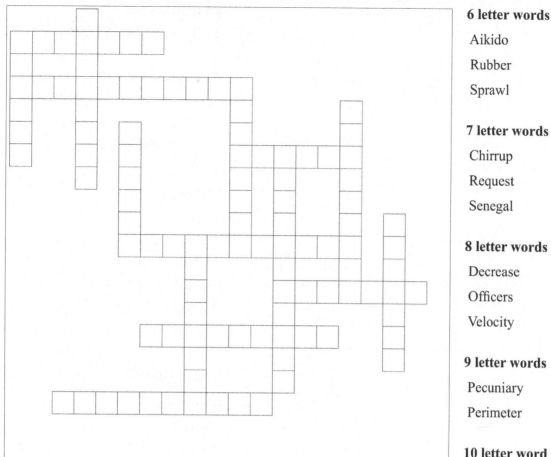

6 letter words
Aikido
Rubber
Sprawl

7 letter words
Chirrup
Request
Senegal

8 letter words
Decrease
Officers
Velocity

9 letter words
Pecuniary
Perimeter

10 letter word
Propulsion

11 letter words
Beneficiary
Oktoberfest
Recommended

Kriss Kross № 54

4 letter word
Boss

5 letter word
Melee

6 letter word
Canyon

7 letter words
Alveoli
Booking
Freezer
Lizards
Tickets

8 letter word
Trinkets

9 letter word
Slingshot

10 letter word
Hesitation

11 letter words
Fundamental
Proficiency

12 letter words
Inexplicable
Interjection

29

Kriss Kross № 55

4 letter word
Desk

5 letter word
Spare

6 letter words
Canals
Motion
Shades

7 letter words
Harvest
Joyride
Tuesday

8 letter words
Blizzard
Humidity
Knitting

9 letter word
Direction

10 letter words
Apiculture
Ecological
Trafficker

Kriss Kross № 56

4 letter words
Avon
Omen

5 letter words
Pause
Robin

6 letter word
Causes

8 letter words
Armament
Brownies
Concrete
Interpol
Playtime
Receiver

9 letter words
Casegoods
Telescope

10 letter word
Burgeoning

11 letter word
Discoveries

Kriss Kross № 57

5 letter words
Court
Waver

6 letter words
Breeze
Grange
Squids
Unused

7 letter words
Airship
Rebirth
Refined
Shyness

8 letter word
Sideline

9 letter word
Wonderful

11 letter words
Approbation
Subtraction

12 letter word
Embezzlement

Kriss Kross № 58

4 letter words
Rose
Vibe

5 letter words
Slaps
Woods

6 letter words
Enzyme
Putter

7 letter words
Shovels
Tipping

8 letter words
Scooters
Speakers

9 letter words
Flattened
Implement
Raindrops
Substance

11 letter word
Cauliflower

Kriss Kross № 59

4 letter word
Germ

5 letter words
Admit
Coupe
Groom
Queue
Waltz

6 letter word
Porter

7 letter words
Catered
Compass
Encrypt
Fluvial
Infants

8 letter words
Flurries
Teaspoon

12 letter word
Substitution

Kriss Kross № 60

4 letter words
Ship
Tart

5 letter words
Germs
Maori
Savvy

6 letter words
Angola
Boxcar
Pedals

7 letter words
Collate
Frailty

8 letter words
Anywhere
Watchful

9 letter word
Indolence

10 letter word
Sanguinary

11 letter word
Discrepancy

Kriss Kross № 61

4 letter words
Reed
Teal

5 letter words
Blade
Extol
Wharf

6 letter word
Attach

7 letter words
Massage
Novella
Replant

9 letter words
Apprehend
Expertise

Staircase

10 letter word
Sustenance

11 letter word
Personalize

12 letter word
Electrolysis

Kriss Kross № 62

5 letter words
Kamet
Milos
Mimic
Pollo

6 letter words
Paypal
Rocket
Soiled

7 letter word
Missive

8 letter word
Croutons

10 letter words
Literature
Madagascar

Perquisite

11 letter words
Earthenware
Fundraising

12 letter word
Congregation

Kriss Kross № 63

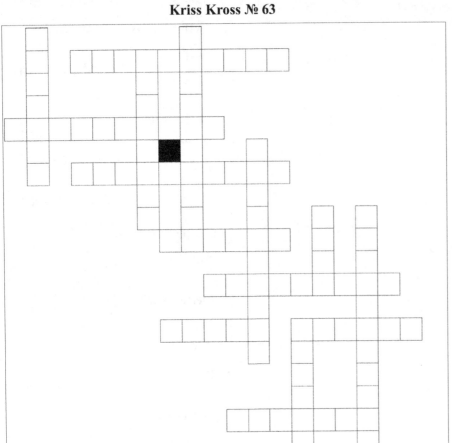

4 letter word
Tips

5 letter word
Novel

6 letter words
Belles
Rodent

7 letter words
Decagon
Germany
Reshape

8 letter word
Eventing

9 letter word
Publisher

10 letter words
Balloonist
Impassable
Medication
Phlegmatic
Volleyball

11 letter word
Independent

Kriss Kross № 64

4 letter words
Gram
Word

5 letter words
Guano
North
Prone
Sunny

6 letter words
Norway
Single

7 letter word
Niagara

8 letter words
Blanched
Carbonic

9 letter words
Affection
Beginning
Perennial

10 letter word
Perception

Kriss Kross № 65

5 letter words
Beets
Gamma

6 letter words
Minced
Streak

7 letter words
Cabinet
Crampon
Handcar
Travels

8 letter word
Cupcakes

9 letter words
Norwegian
Obedience

Watershed

10 letter word
Ecotourism

11 letter word
Deification

12 letter word
Impersonator

Kriss Kross № 66

5 letter word
Minty

6 letter words
Poetic
Tailed
Vendor

7 letter words
Imprint
Locusts

8 letter words
Borehole
Casanova
Cowbells
Maneuver
Ranchers

9 letter words
Banknotes
Hardiness

10 letter word
Micrometer

11 letter word
Chromogenic

Kriss Kross № 67

4 letter word
Plop

5 letter words
Couch
Going
Kinds
Sagas
Width

6 letter words
Browse
Estate
Toxins

7 letter words
Catches
Galileo

10 letter words
Conversion
Monotheism

11 letter word
Interpolate

12 letter word
Replacements

Kriss Kross № 68

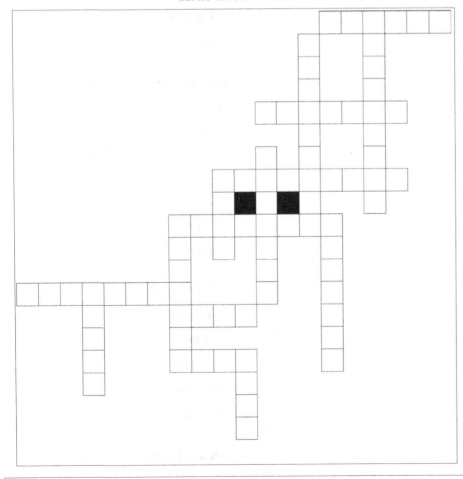

4 letter words
Bass
Leaf
Port
Tact

5 letter word
Steed

6 letter word
Grotto

7 letter words
Develop
Ikebana
Outrank
Treacle

8 letter words
Discreet
Mudslide

9 letter words
Adjective
Boutiques
Organized

Kriss Kross № 69

4 letter words
Clam
Mail

5 letter words
Adler
Jetty
Knack
Maple

6 letter word
Mastic

7 letter words
Cameria
Scaling
Transit

8 letter words
Dinosaur

Reporter

10 letter word
Tiebreaker

11 letter words
Handicrafts
Intentional

Kriss Kross № 70

4 letter word
Park

5 letter words
Denim
Gleam

6 letter words
Frugal
Wattle

7 letter words
Aerogel
Bobsled
Dutiful
Outside

8 letter words
Fraction
Hypnosis

9 letter words
Hibernate
Mythology
Scallions

11 letter word
Commitments

Kriss Kross № 71

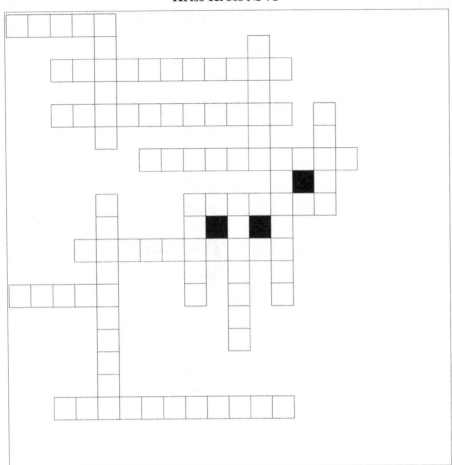

5 letter words
Bloom
Omega
Usage
Venus

6 letter words
Cotton
Masses

7 letter words
Genteel
Outings
Tracing

10 letter words
Chokeberry
Congregate
Upbringing

11 letter words
Crystallize
Dysfunction
Flexibility

Kriss Kross № 72

4 letter words
Diva
Tied

6 letter words
Genome
Pounce
Thighs

7 letter words
Jackson
Mindset

8 letter words
Carapace
Catering
Horsemen
Hostelry
Inventor

9 letter word
Barometer

11 letter word
Pomegranate

12 letter word
Truthfulness

Kriss Kross № 73

6 letter words
Ballad
Choose
Fiance

7 letter words
Arrival
Dawning
Heavens
Serious
Siberia

8 letter words
Amicably
Honeybee
Particle

9 letter words
Originate

Rebellion
Stretcher

11 letter word
Painstaking

Kriss Kross № 74

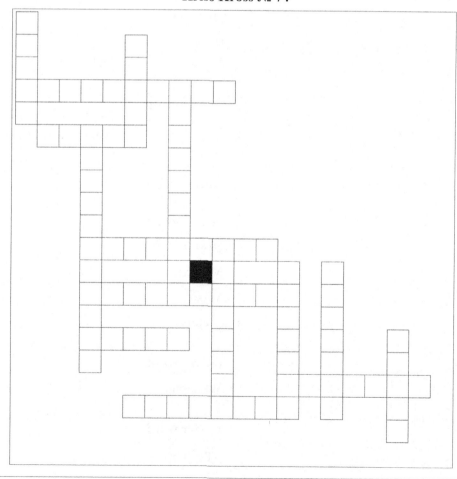

5 letter words
Items
Reply
Stone
Unity
Volta

7 letter words
Agility
Repaper
Thermos

8 letter words
Addition
Friendly

9 letter word
Sideboard

10 letter words
Pretending
Techniques
Unbeatable

11 letter word
Philosophic

Kriss Kross № 75

5 letter words
Align
Roped
Shape
Wages

6 letter words
Brides
Crater
Equipe
Retail
Shower

7 letter words
Croatia
Puddles

8 letter word
Whiplash

9 letter word
Hilarious

10 letter words
Courageous
Generosity

Kriss Kross № 76

5 letter words
Boxed
Stamp

6 letter words
Baltic
Pointe
Salary

7 letter words
Dismiss
Minaret
Varsity
Victory

8 letter word
Whopping

9 letter word
Uplifting

10 letter words
Conveyance
Observance
Pyramiding
Rhinoceros

Kriss Kross № 77

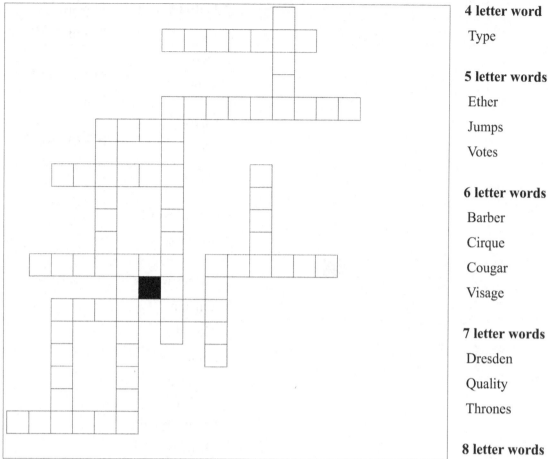

4 letter word
Type

5 letter words
Ether
Jumps
Votes

6 letter words
Barber
Cirque
Cougar
Visage

7 letter words
Dresden
Quality
Thrones

8 letter words
Catapult
Drainage

9 letter word
Flowering

11 letter word
Ferruginous

Kriss Kross № 78

6 letter words
Ballet
Careen
Recent

7 letter words
Empathy
Fortify
Reducer

8 letter words
Duisburg
Foraging
Stimulus

9 letter words
Desperado
Gradation

10 letter word
Acceptance

11 letter words
Discernment
Participate

12 letter word
Preservation

Kriss Kross № 79

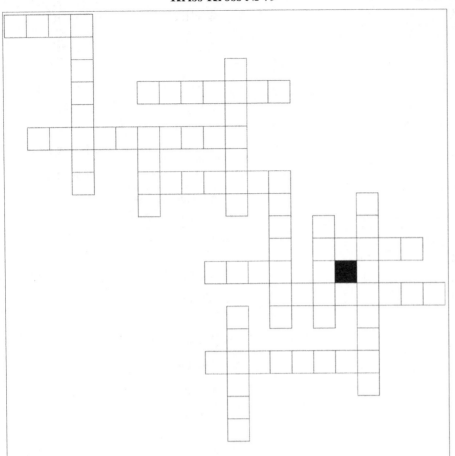

4 letter words
Card
Herb
Lent

5 letter words
Hippo
Image

6 letter word
Amends

7 letter words
Calcium
Hounded
Lullaby
Retouch

8 letter words
Benefits

Exponent
Terminal

9 letter word
Stainless

10 letter word
Xenophobic

Kriss Kross № 80

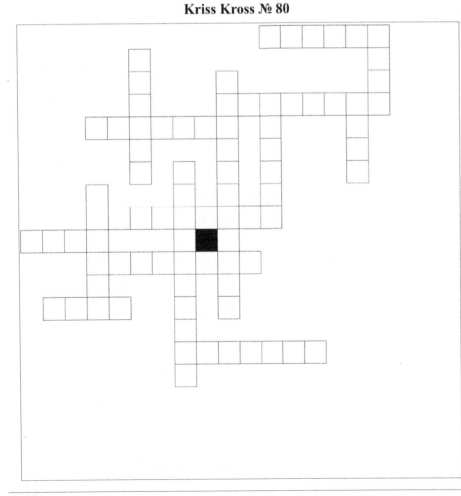

4 letter words
Quad
Rays
Tong
Tray

6 letter words
Hidden
Merlin
Pantry
Salver

7 letter words
Carving
Outline

8 letter words
Download
Remnants

9 letter word
Injection

10 letter word
Excellence

11 letter word
Predominate

Kriss Kross № 81

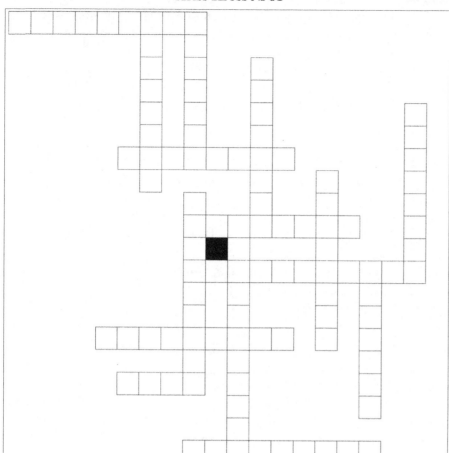

4 letter word
Yarn

7 letter words
Barrage
Objects

8 letter words
Founding
Isotopes
Licenses
Original
Quantify
Renegade

9 letter words
Appealing
Dedicated
Nightclub

Porcelain

11 letter words
Collections
Illuminated

Kriss Kross № 82

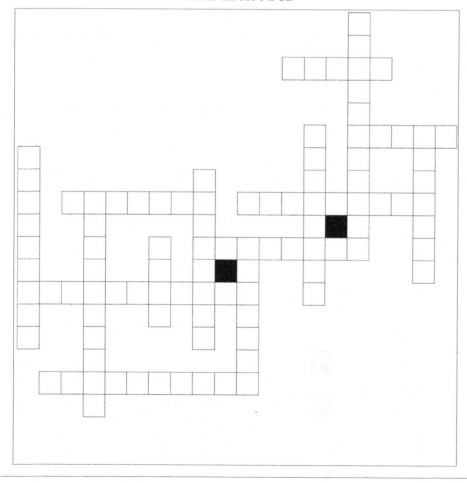

4 letter word
Scan

5 letter words
Blond
Feral

7 letter words
Aquifer
Feather
Lineage

8 letter words
Braiding
Colonize
Traction

9 letter words
Antipasti
Pronounce

10 letter words
Employment
Innumerate

11 letter words
Negotiation
Pontificate

Kriss Kross № 83

4 letter words
Crew
Judo

5 letter words
Bombe
Creel
Sable
Serum
Traje

6 letter words
Billet
Brands
Duress
Fridge

7 letter word
Snowman

9 letter word
Snapshots

10 letter word
Newfangled

11 letter word
Termination

Kriss Kross № 84

6 letter word
Latvia

7 letter word
Betting

8 letter words
Dominate
Speaking
Underarm
Unsolved

9 letter words
Reception
Spectator

10 letter words
Broadening
Personable
Scratching

11 letter words
Equivalency
Territorial
Vindication

12 letter word
Freewheeling

Kriss Kross № 85

4 letter words
Cups
Haul
Swap
Tech

6 letter word
Adroit

7 letter words
Academy
Oversee
Reading
Reasons
Regatta
Seizure

8 letter words
Suitcase

Textiles

9 letter word
Harmonium

11 letter word
Crystalline

Kriss Kross № 86

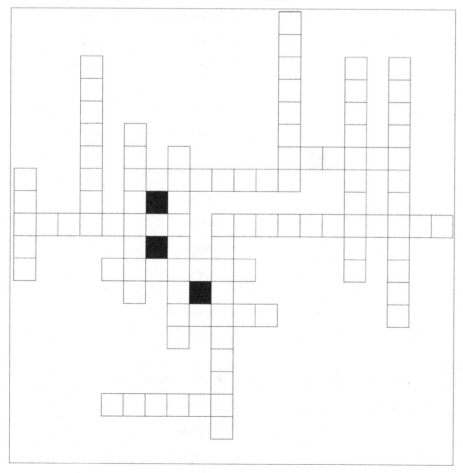

5 letter words
Alike
Drama

6 letter words
Dawson
Nectar

7 letter word
Busting

8 letter words
Allspice
Bustling
Mystique
Pilgrims
Spending

9 letter word
Celestial

10 letter words
Convincing
Excitement

11 letter word
Carburettor

12 letter word
Distractions

Kriss Kross № 87

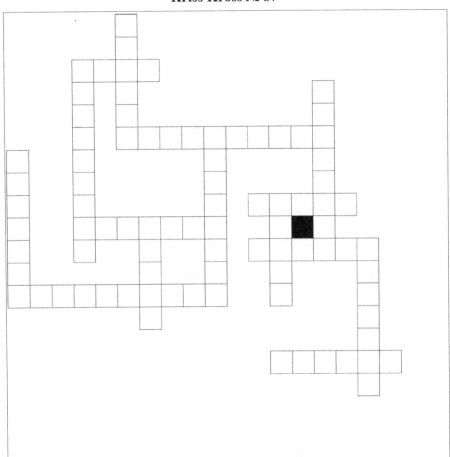

4 letter word
Salt

5 letter words
Early
Float
Lucia

6 letter words
Folded
Sculpt
Scutes

7 letter words
Deficit
Roselle
Tracker

8 letter words
Baseball

Heavenly

9 letter word
Stevedore

10 letter words
Diaphanous
Toxicology

Kriss Kross № 88

4 letter words
Paid
Seat

5 letter word
Gulch

6 letter words
Basalt
Carols
Dances
Device

7 letter word
Leafing

8 letter words
Abundant
Applause
Chemical

Contests
Thatched
Vigorous

9 letter word
Landscape

Kriss Kross № 89

4 letter words
Doer
Grit
Milk

5 letter words
Games
Homer

6 letter words
Health
Sheets

7 letter words
Idolise
Teeming

8 letter words
Countess
Geometry

Wanderer

9 letter words
Expansive
Intervals

11 letter word
Fascination

Kriss Kross № 90

5 letter word
Trial

6 letter words
Embryo
Matrix

7 letter words
Jerseys
Lending
Telling

8 letter words
Amenable
Lemonade
Penciled

9 letter words
Avocation
Portfolio

Wandering

10 letter words
Centennial
Cornflower

11 letter word
Educational

Kriss Kross № 91

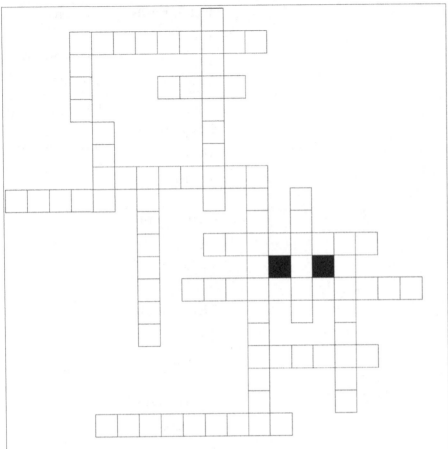

4 letter words
Exit
John
Slim

5 letter word
Glean

6 letter words
Saline
Tribal

8 letter words
Hispanic
Resolute
Standard
Tertiary

9 letter words
Bloodline

Elevation
Finishing

11 letter word
Mercenaries

12 letter word
Consecration

Kriss Kross № 92

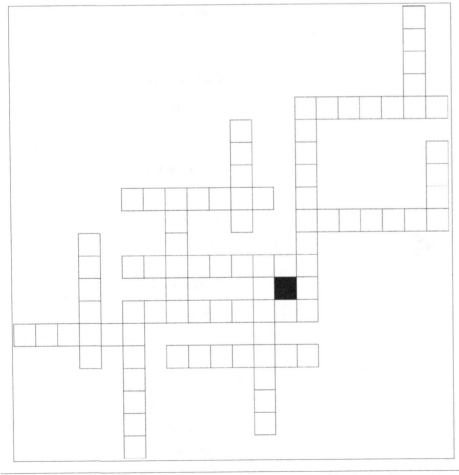

4 letter word
Mike

5 letter words
Dodge
Match

6 letter words
Cutlet
Folate
Frills

7 letter words
Emitter
Infancy
Notable
Stanley
Thrifty

8 letter word

Overflow

9 letter words
Grandiose
Specimens

10 letter word
Encounters

Kriss Kross № 93

4 letter words
Dean
Mule
Riot

5 letter words
Gifts
Prima

6 letter words
Armies
Geckos

7 letter words
Caracas
Ecology
Remarks
Spindle

8 letter word
Nutrient

9 letter words
Submerged
Valuables

11 letter word
Maintenance

Kriss Kross № 94

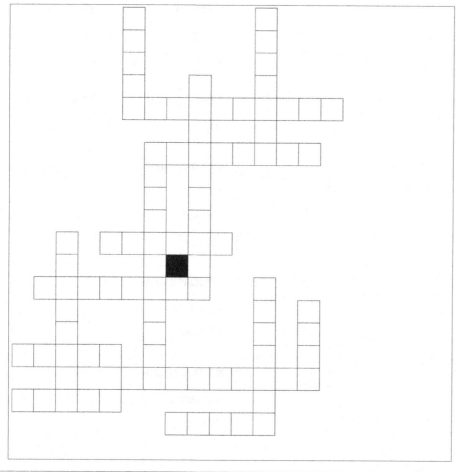

4 letter word
Jews

5 letter words
Anita
Natal
Press
Smile

6 letter word
Oregon

7 letter words
Auditor
Termite

8 letter words
Glibness
Hillside
Pedigree

9 letter word
Arachnids

10 letter words
Conditions
Locomotive

11 letter word
Predecessor

Kriss Kross № 95

4 letter words
Axel
Flip
York

5 letter word
Puree

6 letter words
Elbert
Engine
Shirts
Spritz

7 letter words
Density
Immense
Kindred

8 letter word
Offshoot

10 letter words
Analytical
Roundhouse

12 letter word
Nomenclature

Kriss Kross № 96

4 letter words
Coop
Post

5 letter word
Mines

6 letter words
Brooch
Height
Panels

7 letter words
Healthy
Odyssey

8 letter words
Flossing
Petition

9 letter words
Condition
Shellfish

10 letter words
Centimeter
Headhunter
Provenance

Kriss Kross № 97

4 letter word
Dyes

5 letter words
Award
Party
Solid

6 letter words
Copper
Endure
Mainly
Marred

7 letter word
Cumulus

8 letter words
Oenology
Sociable

9 letter words
Freewheel
Limitless
Presently

10 letter word
Nonfiction

Kriss Kross № 98

4 letter words
Rica
Tuba

6 letter words
Packet
Parker
Ripple

7 letter words
Aerosol
Olympic
Overbid

8 letter words
Aromatic
Membrane

9 letter word
Ferocious

10 letter words
Delegation
Governance
Turbulence

12 letter word
Unemployment

Kriss Kross № 99

4 letter word
Fill

5 letter words
Erupt
Glitz
Peaks

6 letter words
Fabric
Ginger
Saucer

7 letter word
Insight

8 letter words
Commands
Delicacy
Lyricist

Princess
Response

9 letter words
Constancy
Outnumber

Kriss Kross № 100

4 letter words
Host
Perk

5 letter words
Brass
China

6 letter words
Sparta
Stored
Tactic

7 letter word
Physics

8 letter words
Airlines
Familial
Sprinkle

9 letter word
Husbandry

10 letter word
Witchcraft

11 letter words
Antioxidant
Uncollected

Solutions

Kriss Kross № 1

Kriss Kross № 2

Kriss Kross № 3

Kriss Kross № 4

Kriss Kross № 5
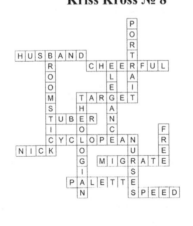

Kriss Kross № 6
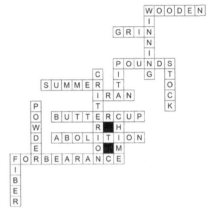

Kriss Kross № 7

Kriss Kross № 8
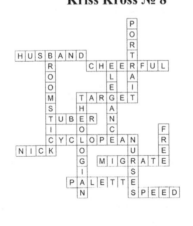

Kriss Kross № 9

Kriss Kross № 10
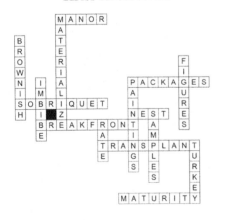

Kriss Kross № 11
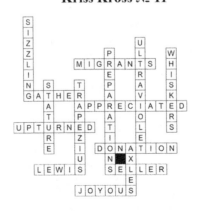

Kriss Kross № 12
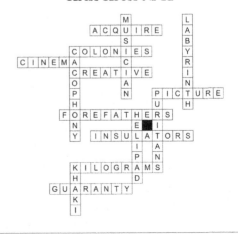

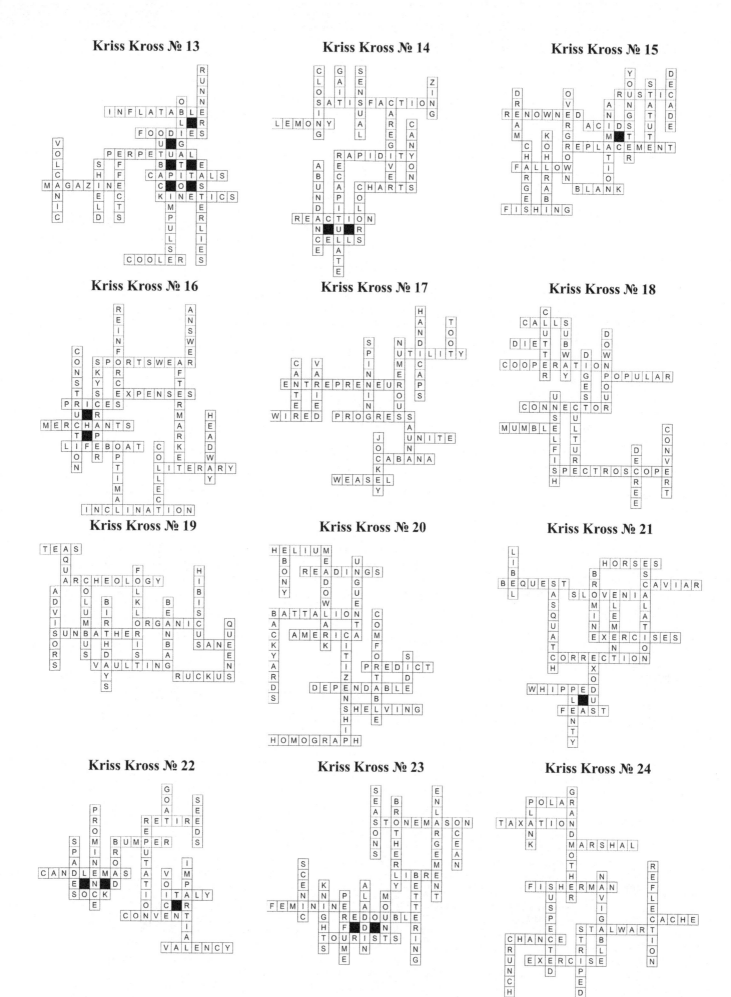

Kriss Kross № 25
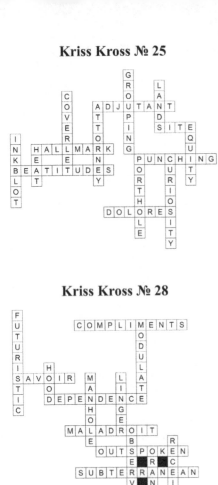

Kriss Kross № 26

Kriss Kross № 27
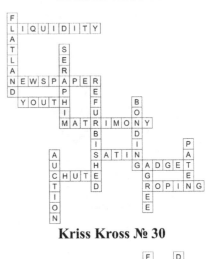

Kriss Kross № 28

Kriss Kross № 29

Kriss Kross № 30

Kriss Kross № 31
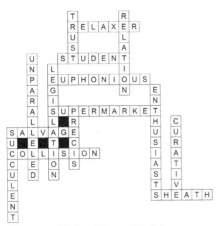

Kriss Kross № 32
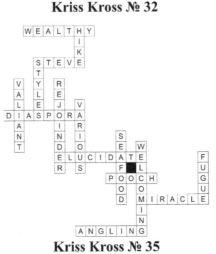

Kriss Kross № 33
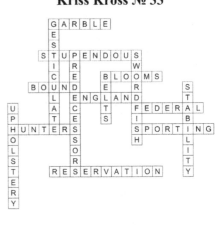

Kriss Kross № 34
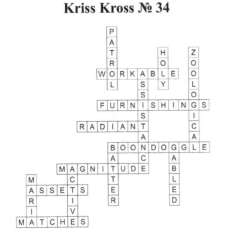

Kriss Kross № 35

Kriss Kross № 36
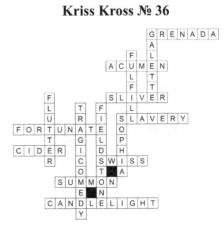

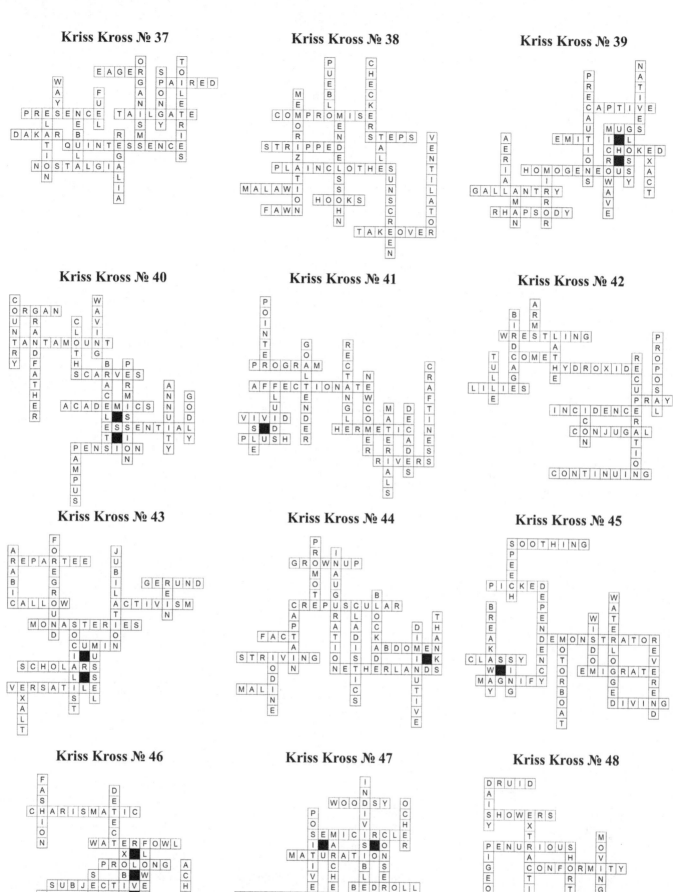

Kriss Kross № 49

Kriss Kross № 50

Kriss Kross № 51
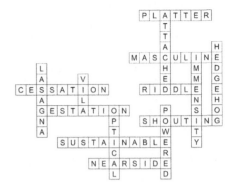

Kriss Kross № 52
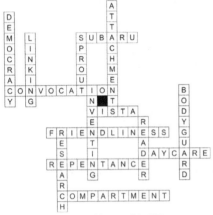

Kriss Kross № 53
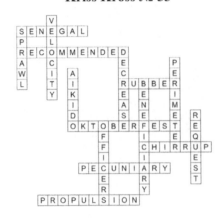

Kriss Kross № 54
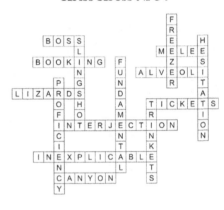

Kriss Kross № 55
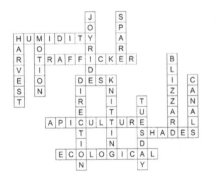

Kriss Kross № 56

Kriss Kross № 57

Kriss Kross № 58
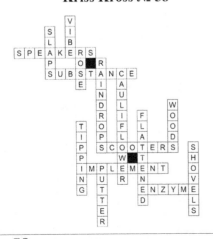

Kriss Kross № 59
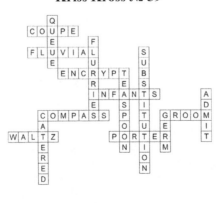

Kriss Kross № 60
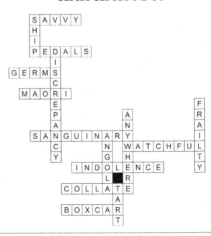

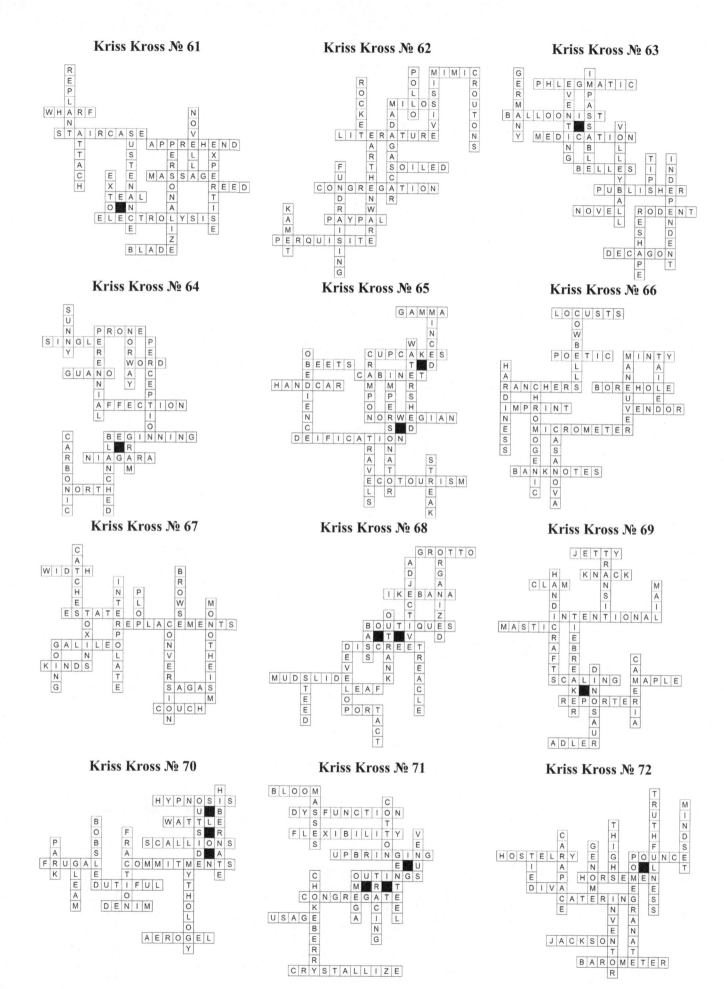

Kriss Kross № 73

Kriss Kross № 74
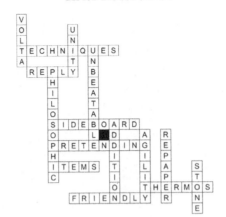

Kriss Kross № 75

Kriss Kross № 76

Kriss Kross № 77
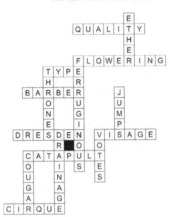

Kriss Kross № 78

Kriss Kross № 79

Kriss Kross № 80

Kriss Kross № 81
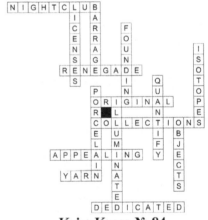

Kriss Kross № 82
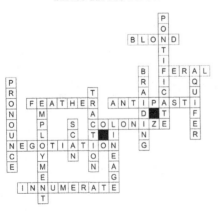

Kriss Kross № 83

Kriss Kross № 84
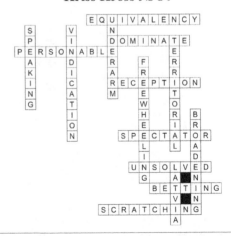

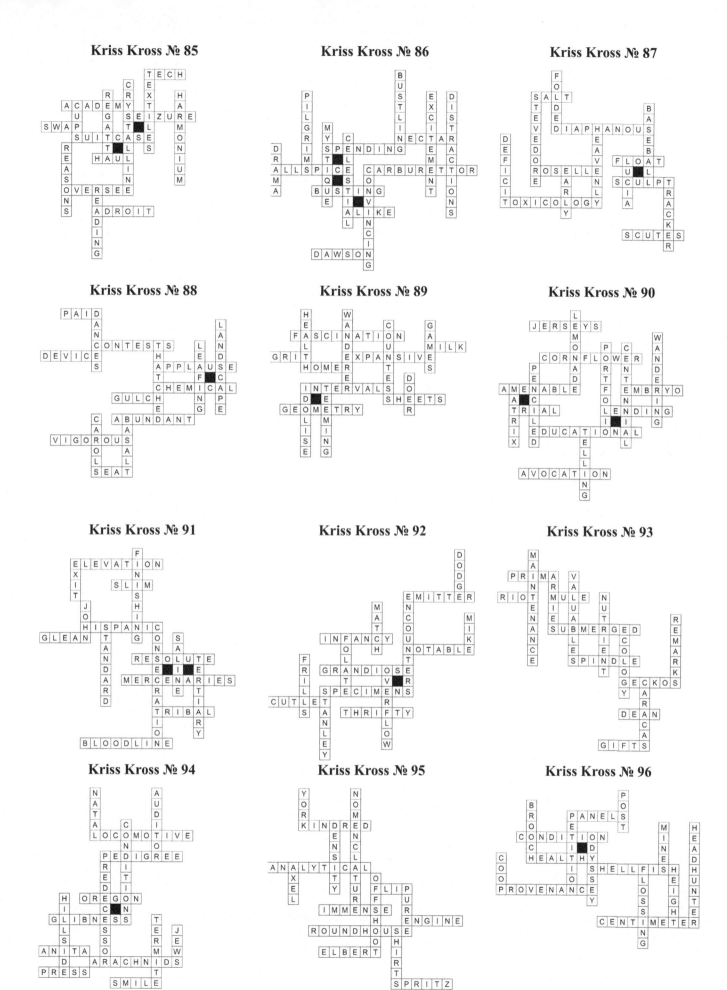

Kriss Kross № 97

Kriss Kross № 98

Kriss Kross № 99

Kriss Kross № 100

Made in the USA
Middletown, DE
21 February 2024

50133137R00038